Disney Theatrical Productions
under the direction of
Thomas Schumacher
presents

BROADWAY'S NEW MUSICAL COMEDY

Music by	*Lyrics by*	*Book by*
ALAN MENKEN	**HOWARD ASHMAN**	**CHAD BEGUELIN**
	TIM RICE and CHAD BEGUELIN	

Based on the Disney film written by RON CLEMENTS, JOHN MUSKER, TED ELLIOTT & TERRY ROSSIO and directed and produced by JOHN MUSKER & RON CLEMENTS

Starring
ADAM JACOBS

JAMES MONROE IGLEHART   COURTNE...

BRIAN GONZALEZ   **BRANDON O'NEILL**   JON...

CLIFTON DAVIS   **DON DARRYL RIVE...**

MERWIN FOARD   **MICHAEL JAMES S...**

and
JONATHAN FREEMAN
as "Jafar"

TIA ALTINAY   MIKE CANNON   ANDREW CAO   LAURYN CIARDULLO   JOSHUA DELA CRUZ
YUREL ECHEZARRETA   DAISY HOBBS   DONALD JONES, JR.   ADAM KAOKEPT   NIKKI LONG   STANLEY MARTIN
BRANDT MARTINEZ   MICHAEL MINDLIN   RHEA PATTERSON   BOBBY PESTKA   KHORI MICHELLE PETINAUD
ARIEL REID   JENNIFER RIAS   TRENT SAUNDERS   JAZ SEALEY   DENNIS STOWE   MARISHA WALLACE   BUD WEBER

Associate Producer	*Technical Supervision*	*Production Supervisor*
ANNE QUART	**GEOFFREY QUART/**	**CLIFFORD SCHWARTZ**
	HUDSON THEATRICAL ASSOCIATES	

General Managers	*Associate Director*	*Associate Choreographer*	*Casting*
MYRIAH BASH	**SCOTT TAYLOR**	**JOHN MacINNIS**	**TARA RUBIN CASTING**
EDUARDO CASTRO			**ERIC WOODALL, CSA**

Dance Music Arrangements	*Music Coordinator*	*Fight Direction*	*Production Stage Manager*
GLEN KELLY	**HOWARD JOINES**	**J. ALLEN SUDDETH**	**JIMMIE LEE SMITH**

Sound Design	*Hair Design*	*Makeup Design*	*Illusion Design*
KEN TRAVIS	**JOSH MARQUETTE**	**MILAGROS MEDINA-CERDEIRA**	**JIM STEINMEYER**

Costume Design	*Lighting Design*
GREGG BARNES	**NATASHA KATZ**

Scenic Design
BOB CROWLEY

Orchestrations
DANNY TROOB

Music Supervision
Incidental Music & Vocal Arrangements
MICHAEL KOSARIN

Directed and Choreographed by
CASEY NICHOLAW

The premiere of *Aladdin* was produced by The 5th Avenue Theatre in Seattle, WA. David Armstrong, Executive Producer & Artistic Director;
Bernadine C. Griffin, Managing Director; Bill Berry, Producing Director.

Cover Artwork © Disney
Production photos by Deen van Meer
Additional photos by Matthew Murphy and Cylla von Tiedemann

ISBN 978-1-4803-9667-8

Walt Disney Music Company
Wonderland Music Company, Inc.

DISTRIBUTED BY

HAL•LEONARD®
CORPORATION

7777 W. BLUEMOUND RD. P.O. BOX 13819 MILWAUKEE, WI 53213

In Australia Contact:
Hal Leonard Australia Pty. Ltd.
4 Lentara Court
Cheltenham, Victoria, 3192 Australia
Email: ausadmin@halleonard.com.au

Visit Hal Leonard Online at
www.halleonard.com

JAMES MONROE IGLEHART

DON DARRYL RIVERA, JONATHAN FREEMAN

ADAM JACOBS, COURTNEY REED

ADAM JACOBS, COURTNEY REED

ARABIAN NIGHTS

Lyrics by HOWARD ASHMAN
Music by ALAN MENKEN

oth - er A - ra - bi - an night!

Fol - low me to a place where in - cred - i - ble feats are rou -

tine ev - 'ry hour or so. Where en - chant - ment runs ram - pant, gets

like A - ra - bi - an days

like A - ra - bi - an days

more of - ten than

like A - ra - bi - an days

more of - ten than

...in a lot - ta good ways.

not are hot - ter than hot...

Ah

not are hot - ter than hot...

Ah

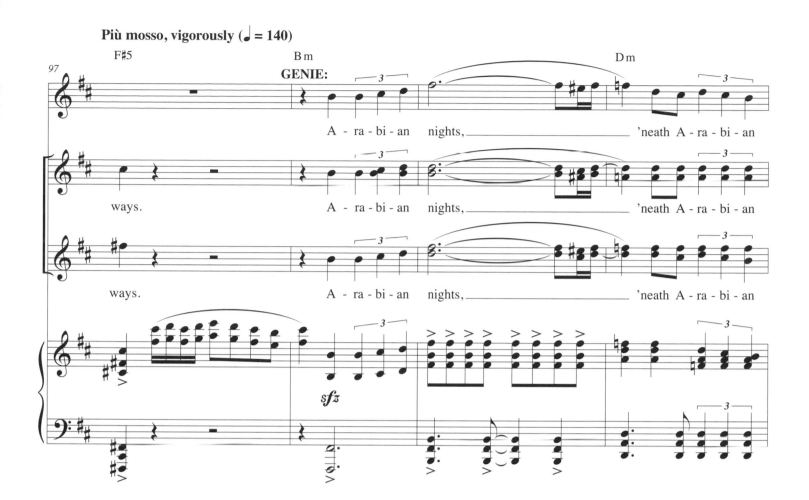

ONE JUMP AHEAD

Music by ALAN MENKEN
Lyrics by TIM RICE

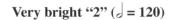

Very bright "2" (♩ = 120)

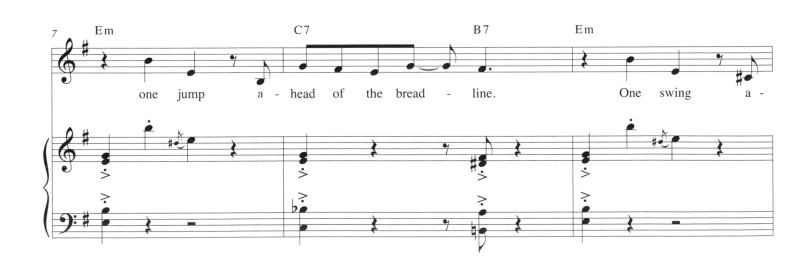

30

ADAM JACOBS

ONE JUMP AHEAD
(Reprise)

Music by ALAN MENKEN
Lyrics by TIM RICE

PROUD OF YOUR BOY

Music by ALAN MENKEN
Lyrics by HOWARD ASHMAN

With determination, poco rubato

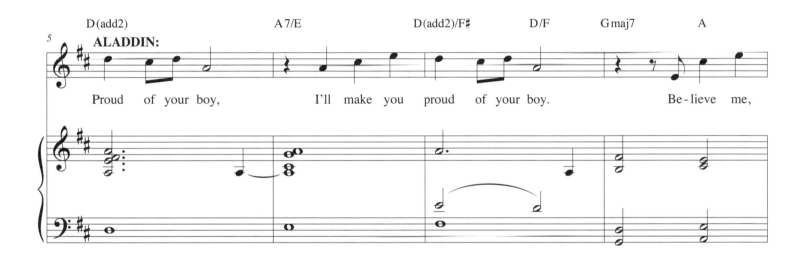

Proud of your boy, I'll make you proud of your boy. Be-lieve me,

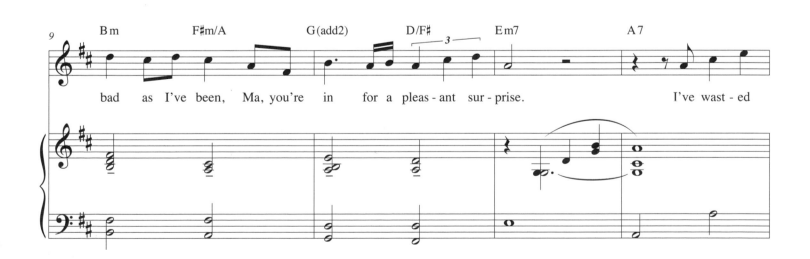

bad as I've been, Ma, you're in for a pleas-ant sur-prise. I've wast-ed

THESE PALACE WALLS

Music by ALAN MENKEN
Lyrics by CHAD BEGUELIN

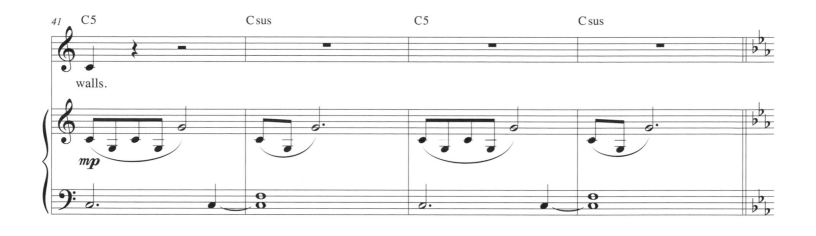

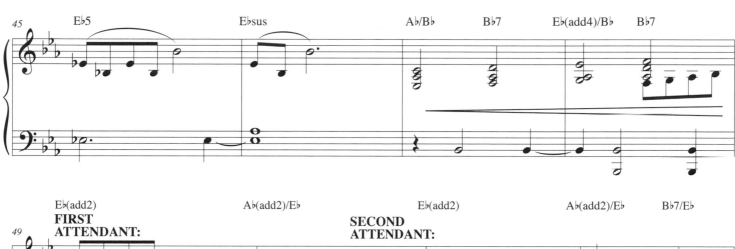

BABKAK, OMAR, ALADDIN, KASSIM

Lyrics by HOWARD ASHMAN
Music by ALAN MENKEN

JAMES MONROE IGLEHART

A MILLION MILES AWAY

Music by ALAN MENKEN
Lyrics by CHAD BEGUELIN

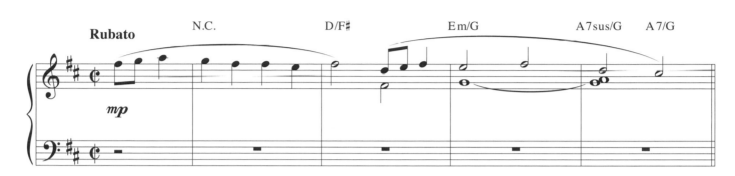

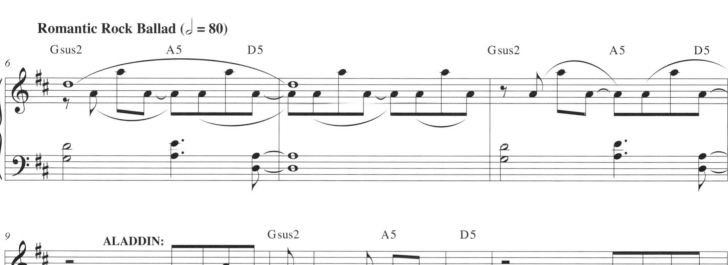

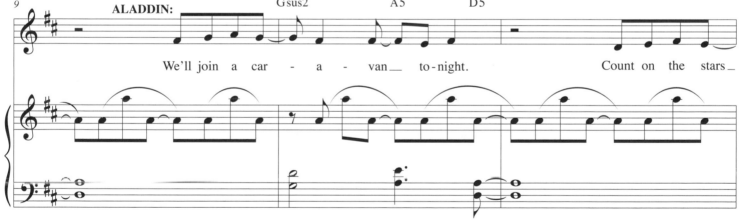

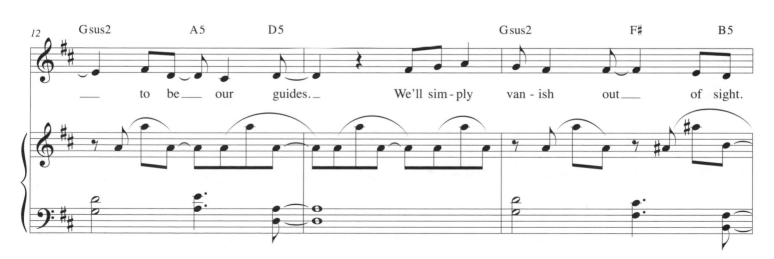

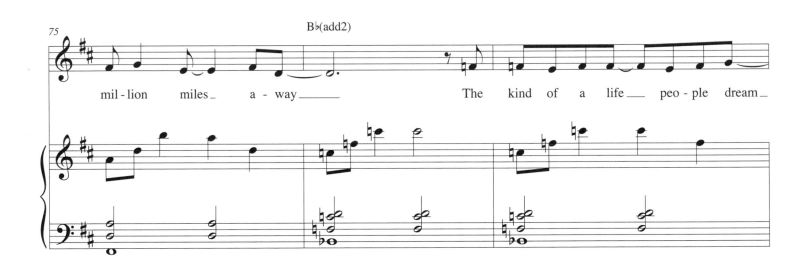

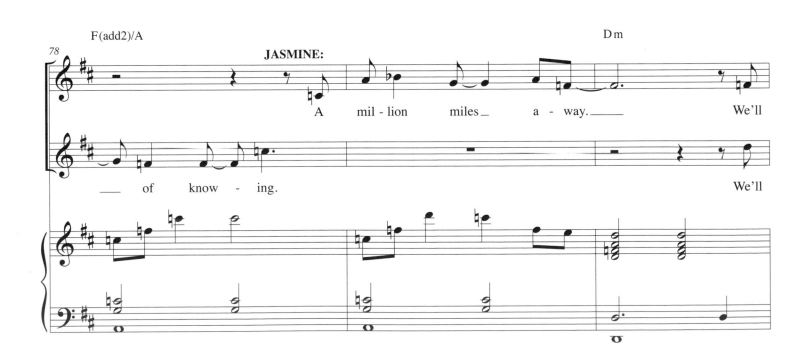

DON DARRYL RIVERA, JONATHAN FREEMAN

DIAMOND IN THE ROUGH

Music by ALAN MENKEN
Lyrics by CHAD BEGUELIN

JAFAR: You have the pro-file of a prince, with a phy-sique that match-es. Be-neath the dirt and patch-es, you are a dia-mond in the rough! I say we work to-geth-er

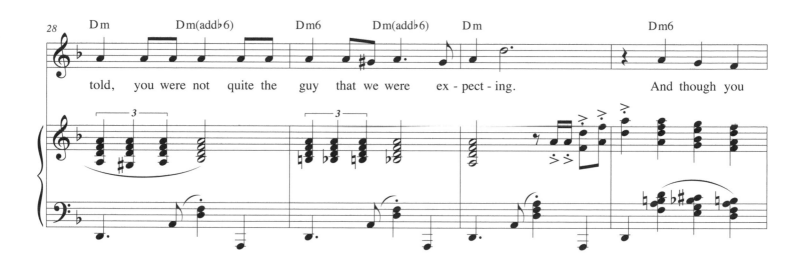

told, you were not quite the guy that we were ex-pect-ing. And though you

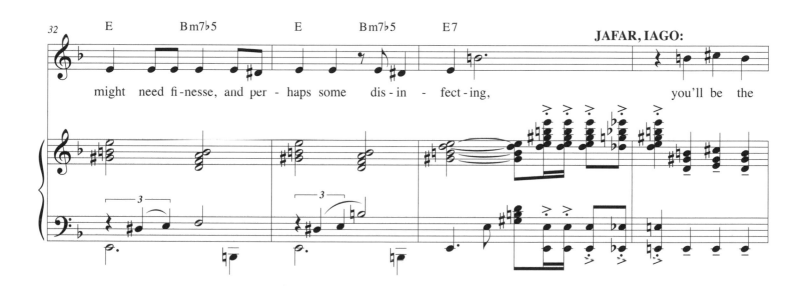

might need fi-nesse, and per-haps some dis-in-fect-ing, **JAFAR, IAGO:** you'll be the

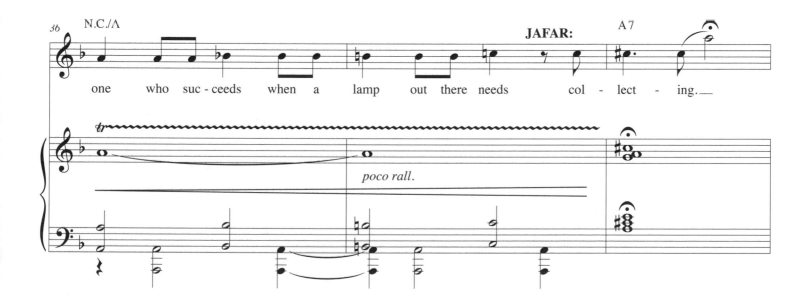

one who suc-ceeds when a lamp out there needs col-lect-ing. **JAFAR:**

rough!

JAFAR:
Look, here's a dia - mond in the...

IAGO:
Three cheers, a dia - mond in the...

Tempo I, con forza

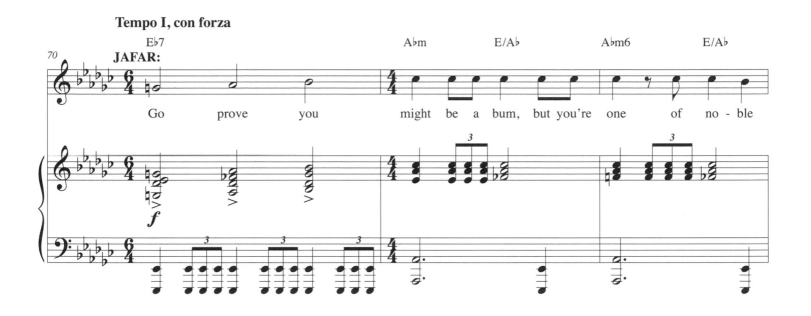

JAFAR: Go prove you might be a bum, but you're one of no-ble

spir - it. IAGO: It's just a cave that might eat you a-

live, no need to fear it. ALADDIN: Well, it's a risk that I might have to

FRIEND LIKE ME

Music by ALAN MENKEN
Lyrics by HOWARD ASHMAN

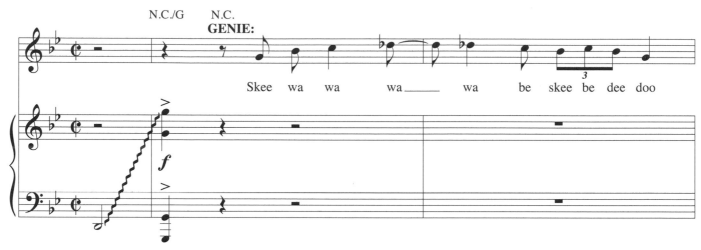

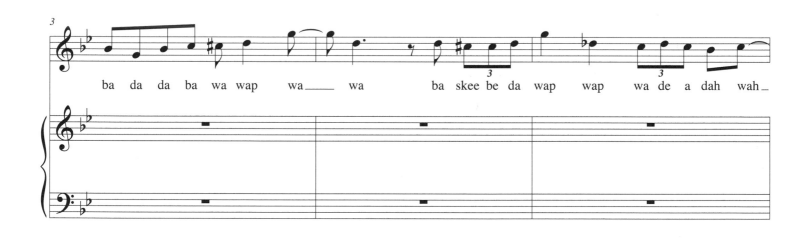

78

PRINCE ALI

Lyrics by HOWARD ASHMAN
Music by ALAN MENKEN

1930s Jazz, Swing 8ths ($\bullet$ = 90)

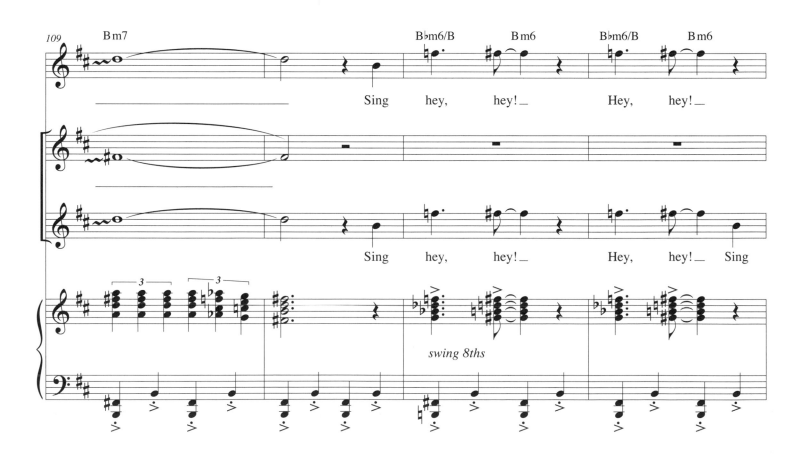

BRANDON O'NEILL, BRIAN GONZALEZ, JONATHAN SCHWARTZ

A WHOLE NEW WORLD

Music by ALAN MENKEN
Lyrics by TIM RICE

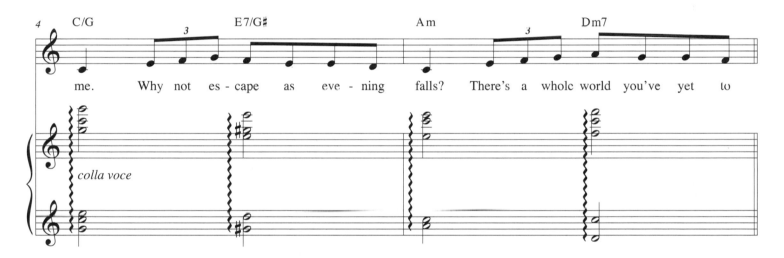

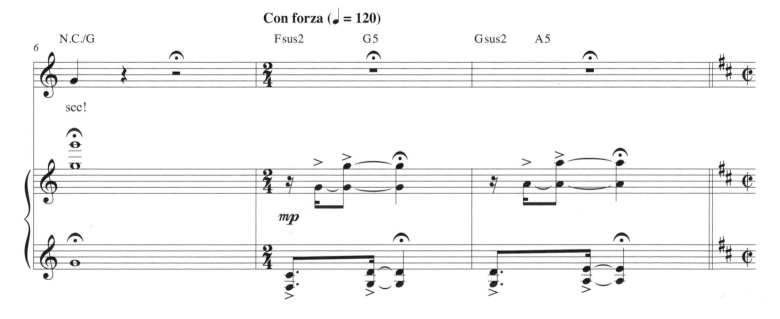

HIGH ADVENTURE

Lyrics by HOWARD ASHMAN
Music by ALAN MENKEN

120

SOMEBODY'S GOT YOUR BACK

Music by ALAN MENKEN
Lyrics by CHAD BEGUELIN

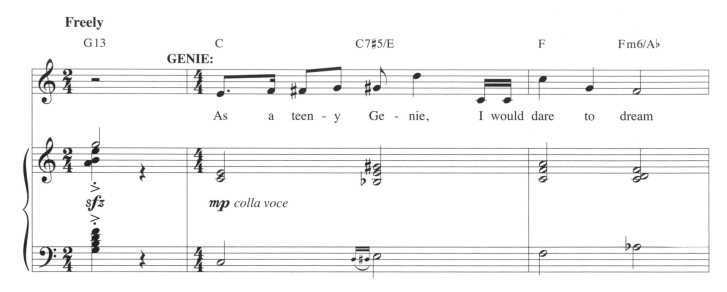

As a teen-y Ge-nie, I would dare to dream

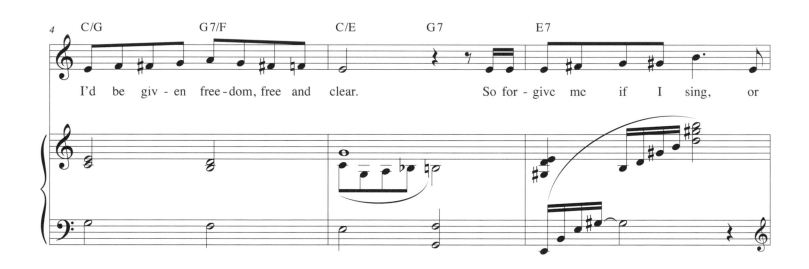

I'd be giv-en free-dom, free and clear. So for-give me if I sing, or

make a whole big thing. But I just can't main-tain my cool ve-neer.